W9-BKZ-692

101 POEMS TO GET YOU THROUGH THE DAY (AND NIGHT)

101 POEMS

TO GET YOU THROUGH

THE DAY (AND NIGHT)

PRESENTED BY

DAISY GOODWIN

Rachel Kohl Community Library
687 Smithbridge Road
Glen Mills, PA 19342

HarperCollins*Publishers*

101 POEMS TO GET YOU THROUGH THE DAY (AND NIGHT). Copyright © 2003 by Daisy Goodwin. All rights reserved. Printed in the United States of America. No part of this book may be used or reproduced in any manner whatsoever without written permission except in the case of brief quotations embodied in critical articles and reviews. For information, address HarperCollins Publishers Inc., 10 East 53rd Street, New York, NY 10022.

HarperCollins books may be purchased for educational, business, or sales promotional use. For information, please write: Special Markets Department, HarperCollins Publishers Inc., 10 East 53rd Street, New York, NY 10022.

Originally published in Great Britain in 2003 by HarperCollins Publishers.

FIRST AMERICAN EDITION PUBLISHED 2003.

Printed on acid-free paper

Library of Congress Cataloging-in-Publication Data

101 poems to get you through the day (and night) / presented by Daisy Goodwin.—1st ed.

    p.   cm.

Includes index.

ISBN 0-06-052912-1

1. Conduct of ife—Poetry. 2. Adjustment (Psychology)—Poetry. 3. English poetry. I. Title: One hundred and one poems to get you through the day (and night). III. Goodwin, Daisy.

PR1195.C62A63 2003

821.008'353—dc21   2003049994

03 04 05 06 07 NMSG/RRD 10 9 8 7 6 5 4 3 2 1

For Marcus and Ottilie

CONTENTS

INTRODUCTION   ix

Getting Out of Bed   1
Stepping on the Scale   7
The Mirror Moment   10
Drivetime   13
Theme Songs   16
Office Politics   20
Blue Period   25
Friends Like These   27
Just Say No   30
System Not Responding   34
Credit Lines   38
Love Struck   41
Separated from the One
    You Love   48
Call Waiting   51
Prescriptions for Life   54
The Parent Trap   58
Battle of the Sexes   62
Escape Routes   69
Off to School   73

Gone Forever   78
Toothache   80
Breaking Up Is Hard to Do   81
Take 5   88
Going Home   91
One for the Road   95
Behaving Badly   97
Going to Bed   101
Not Tonight   110
In the Small Hours   114
Early Morning   119
Weddings   123
Funerals   126
Christmas   129

INDEX OF AUTHORS   131
EMOTIONAL INDEX   135

INTRODUCTION

At first the little things that get you through the day are harmless enough: the extra shot of espresso in your caffe latte, the lunchtime shopping spree, typing your name into an Internet search engine, reading more than one horoscope. Despite this cobweb of little treats, the days (and the nights) seem to get longer, and more serious supports are needed: long drinks shaded by miniature umbrellas, arsenals of painkillers containing codeine, a growing stack of books with titles that are too long to say in one breath—*Men Who Love Women Who Can't Commit on Thursdays*, *Find Your Inner Child and Take it Shopping*, *Feng Shui Your Fridge and Discover the Body You've Always Wanted*. But still the days drag on, more relief is needed: men with sculptured chests and women with implausibly thin inner thighs bang on your door at seven A.M. to take you jogging; you pay people to stick needles into your earlobes; you lie down on a narrow couch covered with an Indian bedspread three times a week and explain to a silent listener why the days still seem too damn long. And yet the ordeal continues; the truly desperate look for oblivion in brown and white powders or drinks with alcohol contents higher than their salaries. But there is an alternative that does not involve writing checks or a phone bill that runs into thousands. The poems in this book offer another way to answer Philip Larkin's question: "What are days for?"

A good poem—the right words in the right order—is human experience at its most concentrated. Open the right poem at the right moment and you will be intoxicated by the distillation of meaning; as its sense unravels you will find it reaching into the nooks and crannies of your mind. As someone who has tried pretty much every way of getting through the day (except of course the illegal ones), I can vouch for the effectiveness of poetry as a powerful antidote to the miseries of modern life. I only wish I'd discovered it earlier—my teenage years would have been considerably more dignified if I had read Wendy Cope's poem "Two Cures for Love":

> 1 Don't see him. Don't phone or write a letter.
> 2 The easy way: get to know him better.

I recommend it as part of any emotional repair kit. Another essential component is Keats's "Ode on Melancholy." I first read it at school where I learned to write knowledgeably on three sides of large sheets of paper about its imagery, but its real meaning eluded me until I had a bout of depression in my twenties and I read it again. What helped me then as much as all the therapy and pharmaceuticals was the poem's central point that melancholy is as much a part of life as happiness and that one cannot exist without the other. Learning to accept that sadness has its own rewards is the quickest and most lasting route to recovery.

But poetry is not only there for the major crises; good poems can smooth away some of life's minor irritations: diets, driving tests, dating. Anyone who wants to be irresistible to the opposite sex has only to read "Siren Song" by Margaret Atwood for the secret: "Alas / It is a boring song / but it works every time." There are poems for ancient miseries like toothache and poems for more modern afflictions such as the computer helpline. But unlike self-help books or long drinks, these poems are not just there to bring instant relief. Keep these words in your head and furnish your mind with beautiful textures, swatches of rich meaning that you can use to illuminate the most dreary situation. You are never alone with a poem.

To help you find the right poem at the right time the book is arranged like a medieval book of hours—those lushly illustrated manuscripts that held an office or prayer for every moment of the day. This anthology starts, logically, with Getting Out of Bed, and then moves on to those other morning traumas: Stepping on the Scale and Looking in the Mirror. As the day moves on there are sections that deal with Office Politics, Off to School, and Escape Routes. And if by five P.M. your head is throbbing, turn to the poems in the Take 5 section and let the world recede. For the reader who is considering having a quick one of whatever variety, there is the Going Home collection to keep you on the straight and narrow; but if it is too late for second thoughts then turn to the Behaving Badly poems, which will equip you with all the excuses you need. If you would really rather go home, but have been inveigled into some unwelcome social activity, then rather than take an assertiveness training course, turn to the Just Say No section. And for anyone who feels vaguely guilty about settling down in front of the TV instead of taking café society by storm then I recommend the poems in the Not Tonight category—"Being Boring" by Wendy Cope in particular.

As part of this survival kit for modern life, I have included poems for the big occasions as well as the small moments. There are poems for weddings, funerals, and even christenings, as well as poems to read when you wake up in the middle of the night drenched in sweat; when the phone just won't ring or when you're seized by dotcom millionaire envy. Not every day is the same thank goodness (if it is you need the Escape Routes section urgently). You might need to refer to the Battle of the Sexes poems on a daily basis, but I hope the Breaking Up Is Hard to Do section is not referred, to very often. For the days when some really big guns are required, try the poems in the Prescriptions for Life and the Theme Songs sections; I always quote the R. S. Thomas line "Live large, man, and dream small," when I find myself in the grip of self-pity.

The poems range from old favorites to previously unpublished works; what they all have in common is that each has something to make the day more bearable. I can vouch for the efficacy of most of the poems in this book personally, but I am also very grateful to all the readers of my last anthology, *101 Poems That Could Save Your Life,* and to its related website www.whatsyourmood.com for all their recommendations. I was delighted, but not surprised, to find that so many people relied on poetry to cure their emotional ailments. I would also like to thank Wendy Cope, Tabitha Potts, Rashna Nekoo, and my daughter, Ottilie, for all their help in compiling this book, as well as the very patient staff at the South Bank Poetry Library.

I hope you will want to read this book at one sitting, but I would urge restraint: poems are like a box of chocolates—you can have too much of a good thing. Better to take these poems little and often, keep this book with you in the spot you would keep your regular crutches: painkillers/cigarettes/mobile phones, and consult it first. Your wallet and your liver will be grateful. And even when your life is running smoothly, have this book to hand to console wounded friends, fortify teenagers through the agonies of adolescence, and reassure captains of industry in mid-life crises. Everyone needs a little help getting through the day (and night).

101 POEMS
TO GET YOU THROUGH
THE DAY (AND NIGHT)

GETTING OUT OF BED

Getting out of bed can be the worst part of the whole day. There are mornings when the slightly stale embrace of the duvet seems irresistible—it's not just a reaction to modern life, the eleventh-century Chinese poet Shao Yung appears to have had the same problem. To remind you of the days when getting up was a joy—the first morning of the summer holidays, for instance—I have included the poems by Browning and Wordsworth. But if those reminders of the joys of living in the present aren't enough, then read the rather grimmer reasons to get the day going provided by Philip Larkin and Arnold Bennett. And if all else fails try the Kipling. Curiosity is the very best reason to get out of bed.

Pippa's Song

The year's at the spring,
And day's at the morn;
Morning's at seven;
The hill-side's dew-pearl'd;
The lark's on the wing;
The snail's on the thorn;
God's in His heaven—
All's right with the world!

Robert Browning

Song on Being Too Lazy to Get Up

Half remembering, yet not remembering, just waked up
        from a dream;
almost sad, but not sad, a time when I'm feeling lazy,
hug the covers, lie on my side, not wanting to get up yet—
beyond the blinds, falling petals fly by in tangled flurries.

Shao Yung,
translated by Burton Watson

My Heart Leaps Up When I Behold

My heart leaps up when I behold
　　　A rainbow in the sky:
So was it when my life began;
So is it now I am a man;
So be it when I shall grow old,
　　　Or let me die!
The Child is father of the Man;
And I could wish my days to be
Bound each to each by natural piety.

William Wordsworth

You Wake Up in the Morning

You wake up in the morning, and lo! your purse is magically filled with twenty-four hours of the magic tissue of the universe of your life. No one can take it from you. No one receives either more or less than you receive. Waste your infinitely precious commodity as much as you will, and the supply will never be withheld from you. Moreover, you cannot draw on the future. Impossible to get into debt. You can only waste the passing moment. You cannot waste tomorrow; it is kept for you.

Arnold Bennett

Days

What are days for?
Days are where we live.
They come, they wake us
Time and time over.

They are to be happy in:
Where can we live but days?

Ah, solving that question
Brings the priest and the doctor
In their long coats
Running over the fields.

Philip Larkin

It's like a book, I think, this bloomin' world,
Which you can read and care for just so long,
But presently you feel that you will die
Unless you get the page you're readin' done,
An' turn another—likely not so good;
But what you're after is to turn 'em all.

from "Sestina of the Tramp-Royal,"
Rudyard Kipling

STEPPING ON THE SCALE

In a recent survey of British women, no fewer than 80 percent of them claimed to be on a diet—fruitlessly, it seems, since 79 percent of the women in the same survey said that when they stopped dieting they regained all the weight they had lost, and more, within six months. If you want an excuse to get off the scales then read Blake Morrison's poem "Against Dieting," but if that does not persuade you that life is too short for *lite* lasagna, then turn to "Feast" by Edna St. Vincent Millay, which advocates the only truly effective diet aid—unrequited love.

Against Dieting

Please, darling, no more diets.
I've heard the talk on why it's
good for one's esteem. I've watched you
jogging lanes and pounding treadmills.
I've even shed two kilos of my own.
But enough. What are love-handles
between friends? For half a stone
it isn't worth the sweat.
I've had it up to here with crispbread.
I doubt the premise too.
Try to see it from my point of view.
I want not less but more of you.

Blake Morrison

Four O'Clock Fantasy

I look at you with lust—so smooth and long,
So firm, cream-filled, yet softening to my tongue,
Your sleek, smooth covering heaven to my eyes.
My conscience pricks. I know I am unwise.

Your sensuous shapeliness invades my soul
With urgent passion to consume you, whole.
In my desire to press you to my lips
I feel you slinking slowly to my hips.

It breaks my heart to leave you lying there . . .
"Yes—how much is that chocolate eclair?"

Yvonne M. Fee

Feast

I drank at every vine.
  The last was like the first.
I came upon no wine
  So wonderful as thirst.

I gnawed at every root.
  I ate of every plant.
I came upon no fruit
  So wonderful as want.

Feed the grape and bean
  To the vintner and monger;
I will lie down lean
  With my thirst and my hunger.

Edna St. Vincent Millay

THE MIRROR MOMENT

These are poems for that moment when you have to confront the gap
between the way you ought to look and the stranger in the looking glass—
an ordeal whose true horror comes through in the Sylvia Plath poem.
There are advantages to growing older, though, "The dog dead and the car
sold," as Roger McGough points out. But if you no longer feel that the best
is yet to come, then read Tennyson's rallying cry to gray panthers
everywhere, "To strive, to seek, to find and not to yield."

Mirror

I am silver and exact. I have no preconceptions.
Whatever I see I swallow immediately
Just as it is, unmisted by love or dislike.
I am not cruel, only truthful—
The eye of a little god, four-cornered.
Most of the time I meditate on the opposite wall.
It is pink, with speckles. I have looked at it so long
I think it is a part of my heart. But it flickers.
Faces and darkness separate us over and over.

Now I am a lake. A woman bends over me,
Searching my reaches for what she really is.
Then she turns to those liars, the candles or the moon.
I see her back, and reflect it faithfully.
She rewards me with tears and an agitation of hands.
I am important to her. She comes and goes.
Each morning it is her face that replaces the darkness.
In me she has drowned a young girl, and in me an old
     woman
Rises toward her day after day, like a terrible fish.

Sylvia Plath

A Joy to Be Old

It's a joy to be old.
Kids through school,
The dog dead and the car sold.

Worth their weight in gold,
Bus passes. Let asses rule.
It's a joy to be old.

The library when it's cold.
Immune from ridicule.
The dog dead and the car sold.

Time now to be bold.
Skinnydipping in the pool.
It's a joy to be old.

Death cannot be cajoled.
No rewinding the spool.
The dog dead and the car sold.

Get out and get arse'oled.
Have fun playing the fool.
It's a joy to be old.
The dog dead and the car sold.

Roger McGough

Old age hath yet his honor and his toil.
Death closes all; but something ere the end,
Some work of noble note, may yet be done,
Not unbecoming men that strove with Gods.
The lights begin to twinkle from the rocks;
The long day wanes; the slow moon climbs; the deep
Moans round with many voices. Come, my friends.
'Tis not too late to seek a newer world.
Push off, and sitting well in order smite
The sounding furrows; for my purpose holds
To sail beyond the sunset, and the baths
Of all the western stars, until I die.
It may be that the gulfs will wash us down;
It may be we shall touch the Happy Isles,
And see the great Achilles, whom we knew.
Tho' much is taken, much abides; and tho'
We are not now that strength which in old days
Moved earth and heaven, that which we are, we are,—
One equal temper of heroic hearts,
Made weak by time and fate, but strong in will
To strive, to seek, to find, and not to yield.

from *Ulysses,*
Alfred Lord Tennyson

DRIVETIME

There are those people who pass their driving test the first time and who spend a lifetime effortlessly reversing into shoebox-size parking spaces, and there are those for whom the driving-test center becomes a second home and who still manage to scrape the only other car in a parking lot the size of Wembley Stadium. Sophie Hannah's poem is for drivers in the second category; having failed the test myself an embarrassing number of times, I find its note of desperation is all too familiar. Betjeman's "Meditation on the A30" is for all those first-time test passers who are clearly responsible for the nation's road rage.

To Whom It May Concern at the Whalley Range Driving Test Centre

Please don't regard this as a threat.
We'll be the best of friends, I bet,
Though up to now we've never met
And I'd just like the chance to get
Some feelings off my chest,

Which won't take very long to read.
The point is this: I must succeed.
I'll never drink and drive or speed.
I really want and really need
To pass my driving test,

And, well, if God forbid I fail
I'll stand outside your house and wail,
Circle your place of work and trail
Black L-plates from a black gauze veil.
I'll be the petrol guest

At every gathering you host,
Proposing a malignant toast,
A sickly, seatbelt-wearing ghost,
Liking you least instead of most.
I'll never let you rest

And may your Fiat Tipo burn.
Sorry. That sounds a little stern.
My nerves are bad. Tonight I learn
Left hand reverse and three point turn
So wish me all the best.

Sophie Hannah

Meditation on the A30

A man on his own in a car
   Is revenging himself on his wife;
He opens the throttle and bubbles with dottle
   And puffs at his pitiful life.

"She's losing her looks very fast,
   She loses her temper all day;
That lorry won't let me get past,
   This Mini is blocking my way.

"Why can't you step on it and shift her!
   I can't go on crawling like this!
At breakfast she said that she wished I was dead—
   Thank heavens we don't have to kiss.

"I'd like a nice blonde on my knee
   And one who won't argue or nag.
Who dares to come hooting at *me*?
   I only give way to a Jag.

"You're barmy or plastered, I'll pass you, you bastard—
   I *will* overtake you. I *will*!"
As he clenches his pipe, his moment is ripe
   And the corner's accepting its kill.

John Betjeman

THEME SONGS

Everybody needs a theme song—a few lines that act as sandbags in times
of trouble, reinforcing self-esteem and keeping the enemy out. My
personal sandbag is the psalm that begins: "I lift up mine eyes to the hills."
I have only to say the first line and the perspective shifts and I can see the
road ahead. I also like the poem by the Welsh poet R. S. Thomas that ends
"Live large, man, and dream small"—uplifting stuff.

I have not loved the world, nor the world me—
But let us part fair foes; I do believe,
Though I have found them not, that there may be
Words which are things, hopes which will not deceive,
And virtues which are merciful, nor weave
Snares for the failing; I would also deem
O'er others' grief that some sincerely grieve;
That two, or one, are almost what they seem,
That goodness is no name, and happiness no dream.

from *Childe Harold's Pilgrimage,*
Lord Byron

I Do Not Speak

I do not ask for mercy for understanding for peace
And in these heavy days I do not ask for release
I do not ask that suffering shall cease.

I do not pray to God to let me die
To give an ear attentive to my cry
To pause in his marching and not hurry by.

I do not ask for anything I do not speak
I do not question and I do not seek
I used to in the day when I was weak.

Now I am strong and lapped in sorrow
As in a coat of magic mail and borrow
From Time today and care not for tomorrow.

Stevie Smith

Say Not the Struggle Nought Availeth

Say not the struggle nought availeth,
    The labor and the wounds are vain,
The enemy faints not, nor faileth,
    And as things have been they remain.

If hopes were dupes, fears may be liars;
    It may be, in yon smoke conceal'd,
Your comrades chase e'en now the fliers,
    And, but for you, possess the field.

For while the tired waves, vainly breaking,
    Seem here no painful inch to gain,
Far back, through creeks and inlets making,
    Comes silent, flooding in, the main.

And not by eastern windows only,
    When daylight comes, comes in the light,
In front, the sun climbs slow, how slowly,
    But westward, look, the land is bright.

Arthur Hugh Clough

Job Davies, eighty-five
Winters old, and still alive
After the slow poison
And treachery of the seasons.

Miserable? Kick my arse!
It needs more than the rain's hearse,
Wind-drawn, to pull me off
The great perch of my laugh.

What's living but courage?
Paunch full of hot porridge,
Nerves strengthened with tea.
Peat-black, dawn found me

Mowing where the grass grew,
Bearded with golden dew.
Rhythm of the long scythe
Kept this tall frame lithe.

What to do? Stay green.
Never mind the machine,
Whose fuel is human souls.
Live large, man, and dream small.

from "Lore,"
R. S. Thomas

OFFICE POLITICS

Offices are like ant colonies, no matter how hard employers try to fiddle with the basic dreary template—introducing innovations like shared desk space, unisex restrooms, and free cappuccino, office workers everywhere are programmed to behave with the same mixture of intrigue and ennui. You can design all the meeting areas you want, but the real hub of the office will always be somewhere else—by the photocopier or on the street corner where the smokers congregate. The American poet Theodore Roethke and the second-century Chinese poet Liu Cheng are good on the monotony of the office; and the poems by Gavin Ewart and Dennis O'Driscoll are reminders that real life is somewhere else.

Poem Without a Category

Office work: a wearisome jumble;
ink drafts: a crosshatch of deletions and smears.
Racing the writing brush, no time to eat,
sun slanting down but never a break;
swamped and muddled in records and reports,
head spinning till it's senseless and numb—
I leave off and go west of the wall,
climb the height and let my eyes roam:
square embankments hold back the clear water,
wild ducks and geese at rest in the middle—
Where can I get a pair of whirring wings
so I can join you to bob on the waves?

Liu Cheng,
translated by Burton Watson

Dolor

I have known the inexorable sadness of pencils,
Neat in their boxes, dolor of pad and paper-weight,
All the misery of manilla folders and mucilage,
Desolation in immaculate public places,
Lonely reception room, lavatory, switchboard,
The unalterable pathos of basin and pitcher,
Ritual of multigraph, paper-clip, comma,
Endless duplication of lives and objects.
And I have seen dust from the walls of institutions,
Finer than flour, alive, more dangerous than silica,
Sift, almost invisible, through long afternoons of tedium,
Dropping a fine film on nails and delicate eyebrows,
Glazing the pale hair, the duplicate gray standard faces.

Theodore Roethke

Success Story

Your name is made.
You have turned the company around,
downsized franchise operations,
increased market penetration
on the leisure side,
returned the focus to core business.
Man of the Month in the export journal,
ruffler of feathers, raiser of dust,
at the height of your abilities.

You don't suspect it yet, but from now on
it will be gradually downhill.
This year or the next you will
barely notice any change—your tan offsets
the thinning of your blow-dried hair,
you recharge your batteries
with longer weekend snooze-ins,
treat back trouble with heat pad and massage,
install an ergonomic chair for daytime comfort.

Behind closed boardroom doors
there will be talk: not quite
the man you were, losing your grip,
ideas a bit blah, in danger
of becoming a spent force.
To your astonishment, the question
of an early severance package comes up
delicately over coffee, low-key as
"Can you pass the sugar, please?"

The flamboyant young blood you trained
starts to talk down, to interrupt
half-way through your report
on grasping brassplate opportunities.
You hear yourself say *In my day*
more often than you should.
Bite your tongue.
Brighten your tie.
Show your old readiness to fight.

Dennis O'Driscoll

Office Friendships

Eve is madly in love with Hugh
And Hugh is keen on Jim.
Charles is in love with very few
And few are in love with him.

Myra sits typing notes of love
With romantic pianist's fingers.
Dick turns his eyes to the heavens above
Where Fran's divine perfume lingers.

Nicky is rolling eyes and tits
And flaunting her wiggly walk.
Everybody is thrilled to bits
By Clive's suggestive talk.

Sex suppressed will go berserk,
But it keeps us all alive.
It's a wonderful change from wives and work
And it ends at half past five.

Gavin Ewart

BLUE PERIOD

When the blues come it is all too tempting to reach for the nearest
panacea, anything to keep smiling. And yet as anyone who has been
depressed eventually finds out, there is a purpose to melancholy. When
the clouds finally lift, you are left with a new appreciation for life—like the
new smells that one notices after a storm. Keats's "Ode on Melancholy"
was recommended to me by an Anglican vicar who herself suffers from
depression: "Prozac and psychotherapy have their place, but they are only
stopgaps—it was reading this poem carefully that made me realize that
sadness was an essential component to enjoying life."

Ode on Melancholy

No, no, go not to Lethe, neither twist
   Wolf's-bane, tight-rooted, for its poisonous wine;
Nor suffer thy pale forehead to be kiss'd
   By nightshade, ruby grape of Proserpine;
Make not your rosary of yew-berries,
   Nor let the beetle, nor the death-moth be
     Your mournful Psyche, nor the downy owl
A partner in your sorrow's mysteries;
   For shade to shade will come too drowsily,
     And drown the wakeful anguish of the soul.

But when the melancholy fit shall fall
   Sudden from heaven like a weeping cloud,
That fosters the droop-headed flowers all,
   And hides the green hill in an April shroud;
Then glut thy sorrow on a morning rose,
   Or on the rainbow of the salt sand-wave,

Or on the wealth of globed peonies;
Or if thy mistress some rich anger shows,
    Emprison her soft hand, and let her rave,
        And feed deep, deep upon her peerless eyes.

She dwells with Beauty—Beauty that must die;
    And Joy, whose hand is ever at his lips
Bidding adieu; and aching Pleasure nigh,
    Turning to Poison while the bee-mouth sips:
Ay, in the very temple of delight
    Veil'd Melancholy has her sovran shrine,
        Though seen of none save him whose strenuous tongue
    Can burst Joy's grape against his palate fine;
His soul shall taste the sadness of her might,
        And be among her cloudy trophies hung.

John Keats

FRIENDS LIKE THESE

Friendship can be as exasperating as it is rewarding: for every thoughtful friend who listens, there is one whose serial misfortunes keep the telephone company's profits healthily plump. I have included here poems for all colors of the friendship spectrum, including poems by Robert Frost and Emily Dickinson on what it takes to be a friend yourself.

> Who, gratis, shared my social glass,
> But when misfortune came to pass,
> Referr'd me to the pump? Alas!
>   My Friend.

from "A Lay of Real Life,"
Thomas Hood

A Time to Talk

When a friend calls to me from the road
And slows his horse to a meaning walk,
I don't stand still and look around
On all the hills I haven't hoed,
And shout from where I am, "What is it?"
No, not as there is a time to talk.
I thrust my hoe in the mellow ground,
Blade-end up and five feet tall,
And plod: I go up to the stone wall
For a friendly visit.

Robert Frost

Friends

They might not need me; but they might.
I'll let my head be just in sight;
A smile as small as mine might be
Precisely their necessity.

Emily Dickinson

JUST SAY NO

Dennis O'Driscoll's poem is for anyone who ever found his or her lips forming the phrase "Yes, I'd love to," independently of their better judgment. The Carol Rumens poem is a reminder of the long-term consequences of "saying the yes you don't mean," and "Tough Triolet" by Wendy Cope is a lesson in the power of "no."

Tough Triolet

(for David Mason)

I had to get tough with Sally Finch.
I told her where to go,
Stood firm and didn't give an inch—
I had to get *tough* with Sally Finch.
And was it difficult? A cinch.
Just kept on saying "No."
I had to get tough with Sally Finch.
I told her where to go.

Wendy Cope

No, Thanks

No, I don't want to drop over for a meal
        on my way home from work.

No, I'd much prefer you didn't feel obliged
        to honour me by staying overnight.

No, I haven't the slightest curiosity about seeing
        how your attic conversion finally turned out.

No, I'm not the least bit interested to hear
        the low-down on your Florida holiday.

No way am I going to blow a Friday night's freedom
        just to round out numbers at your dinner table.

No, I'm simply not able for the excitement
        of your school-term coffee mornings.

No, strange though it may seem, your dream kitchen
        holds no fascination whatsoever for me.

No, there's nothing I'd like less than to get
        together at your product launch reception.

No, I regret I can't fit your brunch into my busy schedule
        —you'll be notified should a suitable opening
occur.

No, I don't appear to have received an invitation
        to your birthday barbeque—it must have gone
astray.

No, my phone was cut off, my e-mail modem caught a
    virus,
        I have run out of fax rolls, note pads, discs,
    papyrus.

No, you can take No for an answer, without bothering
        your head to pop the question.

No, even Yes means No in my tongue, under my breath:
        No, absolutely not, not a snowball's chance, not a
    hope.

Dennis O'Driscoll

A Woman of a Certain Age

"This must have been my life
but I never lived it."
—Her childishly wide stare
at some diminishing reel
of space and brightness, half
illusory, half not,
stuns to an epitaph.
And I can read it all:
how a little lie
whitened to twenty years;
how she was chosen by
something called happiness,
yet nothing, nothing was hers.
And now she has to turn
away, and her bruised eyes
are smiling in their nets:
"It's simple, isn't it?
Never say the yes
you don't mean, but the no
you always meant, say that,
even if it's too late,
even if it kills you."

Carol Rumens

SYSTEM NOT RESPONDING

E-mail, text messages, answering machines . . . modern technology has provided us with so many ways to communicate asynchronously, as they say in geek speak. And yet when the chips are down and the system-error box flashes reproachfully on the screen, you are a slave to the voice at the end of the helpline, a voice speaking from somewhere like Galway or Gothenburg, to bring you relief. As Neil Rollinson points out, "It's like love, this language of DOS,/like talking dirty over the phone." James Fenton's poem is for when another kind of system error occurs and you have to reboot your emotional hard drive and try again.

Helpline

I love your calm, unhurried way, that sexy
lilt in your Irish voice as you take me
line by line through the nightmares
of my Autoexec.Bat and Config.Sys files.
We check the registry for clues,
the boot log, BIOS and System.Ini.
It's like love, this language of DOS,
like talking dirty over the phone.
When I tell you it still won't work
you pause for a moment and moan,
like my hands have found the lush peripherals
beneath your anorak.
Well, you say, it seems your system
is corrupt, you'll have to wipe
your hard disk now and reinstall Windows.
I sigh down the phone. Do you want me
to take you through it? You ask.

You could make invalid page faults
and fatal exceptions sound desirable.
I look at your scribbled name on my pad.
Mary, take me gently, I'm yours.

Neil Rollinson

The Ape at the End of the Phone

I tried to send my love to you
By Electronic Mail.
They returned my Prestel Smoochogram:
Why do I always fail?
I want to blow a kiss to you
But I find my cover's blown.
I'm worse than hit-or-miss to you.
I'm the Ape at the End of the Phone.

They handed me an Apple.
It yielded twenty bytes
And yet I went bananas
When I had you in my sights.
An Apricot was thrust at me
But it only made me groan.
I never thought you trusted me.
I'm the Ape at the End of the Phone.

I lifted the receiver:
There was nothing to receive.
I'm the original Old Adam
And you're the original Eve.
I'm Joseph and you're Mary
And yet I feel alone.
Is it because I'm hairy?
I'm the Ape at the End of the Phone.

I thought that my insistence
Would charm the operator,
But when I order: "Long Distance!"

She tells me to ring back later.
I've tried the gentlest murmur.
I've used a megaphone.
It's a Birmingham number, not Burma.
I'm going Ape at the End of this Phone.

James Fenton and John Fuller

CREDIT LINES

These poems are useful if you've just had your card swallowed up by the hole in the wall. I don't know if the lives of the rich really are as grim as Kate Clanchy claims, but it is a comforting thought nonetheless.

I Would Live All My Life in Nonchalance and Insouciance

I would live all my life in nonchalance and insouciance
Were it not for making a living, which is rather a nouciance.

Ogden Nash

Moderation

He that holds fast the golden mean,
And lives contentedly between
   The little and the great,
Feels not the wants that pinch the poor,
Nor plagues that haunt the rich man's door
   Embittering all his state

Horace, from *Odes, Book II,*
translated by William Cowper

The Rich

This is a note to remind you

that when you envy their lived-in loafers,
the warm tan ankles on ox-blood soles,
when you reach to tip over the chairload
of plump hams in ski slacks, or tighten
the knot of their casual cashmeres—

rise above it, remember

that the men grin grins as if locked in chin-ups,
the women's brows are arched like flautists'.
Their lives are led in pursuit of purpose,
and their eyes are the eyes of a tightrope-walker
who can stride out only, cannot look down.

Kate Clanchy

LOVE STRUCK

If you really are in love then you shouldn't feel guilty wallowing in these poems; if you have got it bad then you won't be able to concentrate on anything else. Enjoy them unconditionally. But if you are in a dry spell or have just put your heart back together then you will appreciate how the Lowell and Beckett poems bristle with menace, and that Wendy Cope's shrink may have a point. Love, after all, *is* a form of psychosis.

Love Is a Circle

Love is a circle that doth restless move,
In the same sweet eternity of love.

Robert Herrick

The Bargain

My true love hath my heart, and I have his,
　By just exchange one for another given:
I hold his dear, and mine he cannot miss,
　　There never was a better bargain driven:
　　　My true love hath my heart, and I have his.

His heart in me keeps him and me in one,
　My heart in him his thoughts and senses guides:
He loves my heart, for once it was his own,
　　I cherish his because in me it bides:
　　　My true love hath my heart, and I have his.

Sir Philip Sidney

The Keyboard and the Mouse

I am myself and in my house
But if I had my way
I'd be the keyboard and the mouse
Under your hands all day.

I'd be the C prompt on the screen.
We could have had some fun
This morning, if I'd only been
Word Perfect 5.1.

I'd be your hard and floppy discs,
I'd be your laser jet,
Your ampersands and asterisks—
I'd be in Somerset

Rotating on your swivel chair.
The journey takes a while
But press return and I'll be there.
Do not delete this file.

Sophie Hannah

The Minute I Heard My First Love Story

The minute I heard my first love story
I started looking for you not knowing
how blind that was.

Lovers don't finally meet somewhere.
They're in each other all along.

Rumi,
translated by Coleman Barks with John Moyne

Will Not Come Back

(After Becquer)

Dark swallows will doubtless come back killing
the injudicious nightflies with a clack of the beak;
but these that stopped full flight to see your beauty
and my good fortune . . . as if they knew our names—
they'll not come back. The thick lemony honeysuckle,
climbing from the earthroot to your window,
will open more beautiful blossoms to the evening;
but these . . . like dewdrops, trembling, shining, falling,
the tears of day—they'll not come back. . . .
Some other love will sound his fireword for you
and wake your heart, perhaps, from its cool sleep;
but silent, absorbed, and on his knees,
as men adore God at the altar, as I love you—
don't blind yourself, you'll not be loved like that.

Robert Lowell

I Would Like My Love to Die

I would like my love to die
and the rain to be falling on the graveyard
and on me walking the streets
mourning the first and last to love me

Samuel Beckett,
translated from the French
by the author

As Sweet

It's all because we're so alike—
Twin souls, we two.
We smile at the expression, yes,
And know it's true.

I told the shrink. He gave our love
A different name.
But he can call it what he likes—
It's still the same.

I long to see you, hear your voice,
My narcissistic object-choice.

Wendy Cope

SEPARATED FROM THE ONE YOU LOVE

Modern life is full of enforced separations—the unmissable career opportunity, the right course at the wrong university. But does anyone left behind believe in their hearts all that talk of the chance of a lifetime? It is only too easy to confuse leaving with rejection. Sophie Hannah's poem "Leaving and Leaving You" should be required reading for both the leaver and the left behind. And then there is enforced absence. I wept when I read "Last Poem" by the French poet Robert Desnos. A hero of the Resistance, he was captured by the Gestapo in 1944. This poem was sent to his wife by a Polish student who found the poet dying of typhus among the survivors of Buchenwald. One can only hope it was of some consolation to the woman Desnos "so fiercely dreamed of."

Westron Wind, When Will Thou Blow

Westron wind, when will thou blow.
The small rain down can rain?
Christ if my love were in my arms.
And I in my bed again.

Anonymous

Leaving and Leaving You

When I leave your postcode and your commuting station,
When I leave undone the things that we planned to do
You may feel you have been left by association
But there is leaving and there is leaving you.

When I leave your town and the club that you belong to,
When I leave without much warning or much regret
Remember, there's doing wrong and there's doing wrong to
You, which I'll never do and I haven't yet,

And when I have gone, remember that in weighing
Everything up, from love to a cheaper rent,
You were all the reasons I thought of staying
And you were none of the reasons why I went

And although I leave your sight and I leave your setting
And our separation is soon to be a fact,
Though you stand beside what I'm leaving and forgetting,
I'm not leaving you, not if motive makes the act.

Sophie Hannah

Last Poem

I have so fiercely dreamed of you
And walked so far and spoken of you so,
Loved a shade of you so hard
That now I've no more left of you.
I'm left to be a shade among the shades
A hundred times more shade than shade
To be shade cast time and time again into your
       sun-transfigured life.

Robert Desnos,
translated from the French by X. J. Kennedy

CALL WAITING

At either end of a love affair the telephone is an instrument of torture. At the beginning each call is weighted with meaning, each telephonic skirmish plotted with military precision. At the end, the answering-machine message is an instantly accessible reminder of what you have lost. But if you have a shred of pride left, remember to withhold your number so those hang-ups can't be traced.

The Pros and the Cons

He'll be pleased if I phone to ask him how he is.
It will make me look considerate and he likes considerate
     people.

He'll be reassured to see that I haven't lost interest,
which might make him happy and then I'll have done him a
     favour.

If I phone him right now I'll get to speak to him sooner
than I will if I sit around waiting for him to phone me.

He might not want to phone me from work in case someone
     hears him
and begins (or continues) to suspect that there's something
     between us.

If I want to and don't, aren't I being a bit immature?
We're both adults. Does it matter, with adults, who makes
     the first move?

But there's always the chance he'll back off if I come on too
     strong
The less keen I appear, the more keen he's likely to be,

and I phoned him twice on Thursday and once on Friday.
He must therefore be fully aware that it's his turn, not mine.

If I make it too easy for him he'll assume I'm too easy,
while if I make no effort, that leaves him with more of a
      challenge

I should demonstrate that I have a sense of proportion.
His work must come first for a while and I shouldn't mind
      waiting

For all I know he could have gone off me already
and if I don't phone I can always say, later, that I went off
      him first.

Sophie Hannah

Siren Song

I phoned from time to time, to see if she's
changed the music on her answerphone.
"Tell me in two words," goes the recording,
"what you were going to tell in a thousand."

I peer into that thought, like peering out
to sea at night, hearing the sound of waves
breaking on rocks, knowing she is there,
listening, waiting for me to speak.

Once in a while she'll pick up the phone
and her voice sings to me out of the past.
The hair on the back of my neck stands up
as I catch her smell for a second.

Hugo Williams

PRESCRIPTIONS FOR LIFE

There are times in the day when we all need a prescription—a reminder of how life ought to be. These poems are guaranteed to make you a nicer person for the next half hour at least. But if you cannot stomach the late Princess of Wales's favorite poem about "Kindness in another's trouble/ Courage in your own," then first read Kingsley Amis's version. And for an instant antidote to self-pity turn to "The City" by the Alexandrian poet C. P. Cavafy; this puts forward the best argument I can think of for doing as you would be done by.

Man's Testament

Life is mostly froth and bubble,
   Two things stand like stone,
Kindness in another's trouble,
   Courage in your own.

Adam Lindsay Gordon

Ye Wearie Wayfarer

Life is largely grief and labour
Two things help you through:
Jeering when they hit your neighbour,
Whining when it's you.

Kingsley Amis

The City

You said: "I'll go to another country, go to another shore,
find another city better than this one.
Whatever I try to do is fated to turn out wrong
and my heart—like something dead—lies buried.
How long can I let my mind moulder in this place?
Wherever I turn, wherever I look,
I see the black ruins of my life, here,
where I've spent so many years, wasted them, destroyed
        them totally."

You won't find a new country, won't find another shore.
This city will always pursue you.
You'll walk the same streets, grow old
in the same neighbourhoods, turn grey in these same
        houses.
You'll always end up in this city. Don't hope for things
        elsewhere:
there's no ship for you, there's no road.
Now that you've wasted your life here, in this small corner,
you've destroyed it everywhere in the world.

C. P. Cavafy,
translated by Edmund Keeley and Philip Sherrard

Common Sense

"There's been an accident!" they said,
"Your servant's cut in half; he's dead!"
"Indeed!" said Mr. Jones, "and please
Send me the half that's got my keys."

Harry Graham

THE PARENT TRAP

These poems are required reading after one of those phone calls from a parent that leaves even the most adult among us speechless with the impotent rage of childhood. But put the phone down gently; one day you will be sorry that there is no one around to treat you as if you were eight years old.

Parents

What it must be like to be an angel
or a squirrel, we can imagine sooner.

The last time we go to bed good,
they are there, lying about darkness.

They dandle us once too often,
these friends who become our enemies.

Suddenly one day, their juniors
are as old as we yearn to be.

They get wrinkles where it is better
smooth, old coughs, and smells.

It is grotesque how they go on
loving us, we go on loving them.

The effrontery, barely imaginable,
of having caused us. And of how.

Their lives: surely
we can do better than that.

This goes on for a long time. Everything
they do is wrong, and the worst thing,

they all do it, is to die,
taking with them the last explanation,

how we came out of the wet sea
or wherever they got us from,

taking the last link
of that chain with them.

Father, mother, we cry, wrinkling,
to our uncomprehending children and grandchildren.

William Meredith

Piano

Softly, in the dusk, a woman is singing to me;
Taking me back down the vista of years, till I see
A child sitting under the piano, in the boom of the
    tingling strings
And pressing the small, poised feet of a mother
    who smiles as she sings.

In spite of myself, the insidious mastery of song
Betrays me back, till the heart of me weeps to belong
To the old Sunday evenings at home, with winter
    outside
And hymns in the cosy parlour, the tinkling piano
    our guide.

So now it is vain for the singer to burst into clamour
With the great black piano appassionato. The
    glamour
Of childish days is upon me, my manhood is cast
Down in the flood of remembrance, I weep like a child
    for the past.

D. H. Lawrence

My Way

I know the difference between right and wrong
I learnt about it at my mother's knee
and all the good belonged of right to her
and all the bad I knew was left to me.

Hers the white innocence behind the veil,
the calm blue passage on the roughest sea
the rose-pink silence and the golden hymn
and hers the comfort of forgiving me.

Mine the red glow of anger, steely tongued,
boredom, green jealousy and black despair,
hatred and envy, pale dreams, purple rage,
the wicked pain of not forgiving her.

I went my way. I knew my way was wrong
and so I feel it every blasted day.
She didn't give me any other choice.
I couldn't leave her any other way.

Dorothy Nimmo

BATTLE OF THE SEXES

I was going to call this section "Sometimes It's Hard to Be a Woman" but male readers have assured me that they have feelings too. Read the poems here with attention and dispense with all those *Men Are from Mars, Women Are from Venus*–type books; if you want the Rules they are all here. You can find out everything you need to know about attracting the opposite sex from Margaret Atwood's "Siren Song." And once the game has started there is sage advice here from Wendy Cope, William Blake, and of course Dorothy Parker on how to keep the ball in play. For long-term success there is the epitaph found in Chelmsford Cathedral, whose author, I suspect, was probably a man.

Siren Song

This is the one song everyone
would like to learn: the song
that is irresistible:

the song that forces men
to leap overboard in squadrons
even though they see the beached skulls

the song nobody knows
because anyone who has heard it
is dead, and the others can't remember.

Shall I tell you the secret
and if I do, will you get me
out of this bird suit?

I don't enjoy it here
squatting on this island
looking picturesque and mythical

with these two feathery maniacs,
I don't enjoy singing
this trio, fatal and valuable.

I will tell the secret to you,
to you, only to you.
Come closer. This song

is a cry for help: Help me!
Only you, only you can,
you are unique

at last. Alas
it is a boring song
but it works every time.

Margaret Atwood

One Perfect Rose

A single flow'r he sent me, since we met.
   All tenderly his messenger he chose;
Deep-hearted, pure, with scented dew still wet—
   One perfect rose.

I knew the language of the floweret;
   "My fragile leaves," it said, "his heart enclose."
Love long has taken for his amulet
   One perfect rose.

Why is it no one ever sent me yet
   One perfect limousine, do you suppose?
Ah no, it's always just my luck to get
   One perfect rose.

Dorothy Parker

Love's Secret

Never seek to tell thy love,
  Love that never told can be;
For the gentle wind doth move
  Silently, invisibly.

I told my love, I told my love,
  I told her all my heart,
Trembling, cold, in ghastly fears.
  Ah! she did depart!

Soon after she was gone from me,
  A traveller came by,
Silently, invisibly:
  He took her with a sigh.

William Blake

He Tells Her

He tells her that the Earth is flat—
He knows the facts, and that is that.
In altercations fierce and long
She tries her best to prove him wrong.
But he has learned to argue well.
He calls her arguments unsound
And often asks her not to yell.
She cannot win. He stands his ground.

The planet goes on being round.

Wendy Cope

Rent

If you want my apartment, sleep in it
but let's have a clear understanding:
the books are still free agents.

If the rocking chair's arms surround you
they can also let you go,
they can shape the air like a body.

I don't want your rent, I want
a radiance of attention
like the candle's flame when we eat,

I mean a kind of awe
attending the spaces between us—
Not a roof but a field of stars.

Jane Cooper

Here Lies the Man Richard

Here lies the man RICHARD,
  And MARY his wife;
Their surname was PRITCHARD,
  They lived without strife.
And the reason was plain:
  They abounded in riches,
They had no care or pain,
And the wife wore the breeches.

epitaph, Chelmsford Cathedral, Essex

ESCAPE ROUTES

These are poems for those moments in the day when the only place to be is somewhere else, when you just want to get going. Read Cavafy's poem "Ithaca" and go on a spiritual minibreak right away. But if you need more practical advice on destinations, try Christopher Logue.

Travel

The railroad track is miles away,
   And the day is loud with voices speaking,
Yet there isn't a train goes by all day
   But I hear its whistle shrieking.

All night there isn't a train goes by,
   Though the night is still for sleep and dreaming,
But I see its cinders red on the sky,
   And hear its engine steaming.

My heart is warm with the friends I make,
   And better friends I'll not be knowing;
Yet there isn't a train I wouldn't take,
   No matter where it's going.

Edna St. Vincent Millay

Ithaca

As you set out for Ithaca
Hope your road is a long one,
Full of adventure, full of discovery . . .

Keep Ithaca always in your mind.
Arriving there is what you're destined for.
But don't hurry the journey at all.
Better if it lasts for years,
So you're old by the time you reach the island,
Wealthy with all you've gained on the way,
Not expecting Ithaca to make you rich.

Ithaca gave you the marvellous journey.
Without her you wouldn't have set out.
She has nothing left to give you now.

And if you find her poor, Ithaca won't have fooled you.
Wise as you have become, so full of experience,
You'll have understood by then what these Ithacas mean.

C. P. Cavafy,
translated by Edmund Keeley and Philip Sherrard

Mountain Talk

I was going along a dusty highroad
when the mountain
across the way
turned me to its silence:
oh I said how come
I don't know you massive symmetry and rest:
nevertheless, said the mountain,
would you want
to be
lodged here with
a changeless prospect, risen
to an unalterable view:
so I went on
counting my numberless fingers.

A. R. Ammons

To a Friend in Search of Rural Seclusion

When all else fails,
  Try Wales.

Christopher Logue

OFF TO SCHOOL

I have a suspicion that Philip Larkin may be right in his gloomy prognosis for the ultimate outcome of the parent/child relationship: "They fuck you up, your mum and dad/They may not mean to, but they do." But as Larkin took his own advice and did not have any children himself, he didn't know the compulsion every parent feels to do the right thing. There are, of course, any number of books that tell you how to be a good parent, but you could save yourself time and money by reading the poems here. I think the extract from "The Prophet" would be a wonderful thing to read at a christening or naming ceremony.

The Mother

Of course I love them, they are my children.
That is my daughter and this is my son.
And this is my life I give them to please them.
It has never been used. Keep it safe. Pass it on.

Anne Stevenson

On Children

... Your children are not your children.
They are the sons and daughters of Life's longing for itself.
They come through you but not from you,
And though they are with you yet they belong not to you.
You may give them your love but not your thoughts.
For they have their own thoughts.

You may house their bodies but not their souls,
For their souls dwell in the house of tomorrow, which you
cannot visit, not even in your dreams.
You may strive to be like them, but seek not to make them
like you.
For life goes not backward nor tarries with yesterday ...

from *The Prophet,*
Kahlil Gibran

For a Five-Year-Old

A snail is climbing up the window-sill
Into your room, after a night of rain.
You call me in to see, and I explain
That it would be unkind to leave it there:
It might crawl to the floor; we must take care
That no one squashes it. You understand,
And carry it outside, with careful hand,
To eat a daffodil.

I see, then, that a kind of faith prevails:
Your gentleness is moulded still by words
From me, who have trapped mice and shot wild birds,
From me, who drowned your kittens, who betrayed
Your closest relatives, and who purveyed
The harshest kind of truth to many another.
But that is how things are: I am your mother,
And we are kind to snails.

Fleur Adcock

Children

If children live with criticism
   they learn to condemn

If children live with hostility
   they learn to fight

If children live with ridicule
   they learn to be shy

If children live with shame
   they learn to feel guilty

If children live with tolerance
   they learn to be patient

If children live with encouragement
   they learn confidence

If children live with praise
   they learn to appreciate

If children live with fairness
   they learn justice

If children live with security
   they learn to have faith

If children live with approval
   they learn to like themselves

If children live with acceptance and friendship
   they learn to find love in the world

Anonymous

GONE FOREVER

I hesitated about including this poem as it is so savage in its grief, a howl of pain rather than a murmur of consolation. But in the first shock of private loss perhaps only a poem as powerful as this will do. For more public expressions of grief turn to the "Funerals" section.

Dirge Without Music

I am not resigned to the shutting away of loving hearts in
      the hard ground.
So it is, and so it will be, for so it has been, time out of
      mind:
Into the darkness they go, the wise and the lovely. Crowned
With lilies and with laurel they go; but I am not resigned.

Lovers and thinkers, into the earth with you.
Be one with the dull, the indiscriminate dust.
A fragment of what you felt, of what you knew,
A formula, a phrase remains,—but the best is lost.

The answers quick and keen, the honest look, the laughter,
      the love,—
They are gone. They are gone to feed the roses. Elegant and
      curled
Is the blossom. Fragrant is the blossom. I know. But I do not
      approve.
More precious was the light in your eyes than all the roses in
      the world.

Down, down, down into the darkness of the grave
Gently they go, the beautiful, the tender, the kind;
Quietly they go, the intelligent, the witty, the brave.
I know. But I do not approve. And I am not resigned.

Edna St. Vincent Millay

TOOTHACHE

With regular flossing you may never need this poem, but it is worth having just in case . . .

A Charm Against the Toothache

Venerable Mother Toothache
Climb down from the white battlements,
Stop twisting in your yellow fingers
The fourfold rope of nerves;
And tomorrow I will give you a tot of whisky
To hold in your cupped hands,
A garland of anise-flowers,
And three cloves like nails.

And tell the attendant gnomes
It is time to knock off now,
To shoulder their little pick-axes,
Their cold-chisels and drills.
And you may mount by a silver ladder
Into the sky, to grind
In the cracked polished mortar
Of the hollow moon.

By the lapse of warm waters,
And the poppies nodding like red coals,
The paths on the granite mountains,
And the plantation of my dreams.

John Heath Stubbs

BREAKING UP IS HARD TO DO

This is the longest section in this book, but for the heartbroken poems are the best rescue remedy—safer and cheaper than gin or lachrymose phone calls to long-suffering friends. I have included Edna St. Vincent Millay's poem that begins "Time does not bring relief; you all have lied," because in the first shock of anguish a month can seem like a century; but remember Millay wrote the poem when she was very young. She, like everyone else, got over it. For really practical advice on how to get over him or her read "Two Cures for Love" by Wendy Cope. When you can read it and smile, you'll know you are over the worst. And when the pain has subsided to a distant twinge read the Yeats and allow yourself a few delicious tears.

> Since that day
> I have not moved the pieces
> On the board.
>
> Jorge Luis Borges

Time Does Not Bring Relief

Time does not bring relief; you all have lied
Who told me time would ease me of my pain!
I miss him in the weeping of the rain;
I want him at the shrinking of the tide;
The old snows melt from every mountain-side,
And last year's leaves are smoke in every lane;
But last year's bitter loving must remain
Heaped on my heart, and my old thoughts abide!
There are a hundred places where I fear
To go,—so with his memory they brim!
And entering with relief some quiet place
Where never fell his foot or shone his face
I say, 'There is no memory of him here!'
And so stand stricken, so remembering him.

Edna St. Vincent Millay

Defining the Problem

I can't forgive you. Even if I could
You wouldn't pardon me for seeing through you.
And yet I cannot cure myself of love
For what I thought you were before I knew you.

Wendy Cope

All That

And then there's the one you write
that makes even you laugh.
You never want to see her again.
You don't want to see her handwriting
on a letter. You don't want to come home
and see the little yellow light
flashing messages of regret.
You don't want to pick up the phone
and hear how much she's been missing you.
Couldn't you meet for a drink?
Not any more. Maybe in a year or two.
All you want to do now
is draw a line under your life
and get on with the past.
Do you make yourself perfectly clear?
You sign with just your name,
a businesslike touch
which makes even you laugh.

Hugo Williams

Quick and Bitter

The end was quick and bitter.
Slow and sweet was the time between us,
slow and sweet were the nights
when my hands did not touch one another in despair
but in the love of your body
which came between them.

And when I entered into you
it seemed then that great happiness
could be measured with the precision
of sharp pain. Quick and bitter.

Slow and sweet were the nights.
Now is bitter and grinding as sand—
"Let's be sensible" and similar curses.

And as we stray further from love
we multiply the words,
words and sentences so long and orderly.
Had we remained together
we could have become a silence.

Yehuda Amichai,
translated from the Hebrew by Assia Gutmann

Two Cures for Love

1 Don't see him. Don't phone or write a letter.
2 The easy way: get to know him better.

Wendy Cope

When You Are Old

When you are old and gray and full of sleep
　And nodding by the fire, take down this book,
　And slowly read, and dream of the soft look
Your eyes had once, and of their shadows deep;

How many loved your moments of glad grace,
　And loved your beauty with love false or true;
　But one man loved the pilgrim soul in you,
And loved the sorrows of your changing face.

And bending down beside the glowing bars,
　Murmur, a little sadly, how love fled
　And paced upon the mountains overhead,
And hid his face amid a crowd of stars.

W. B. Yeats

TAKE 5

These poems are for the point in the day when your head is throbbing with accumulated frustrations: parking tickets, snowdrifts of Post-it notes, supermarket baskets with shaky wheels, road repairs, voicemail . . . Before you do something drastic, drop your shoulders and let these poems put things in perspective. Easier on the joints than yoga.

> What wondrous life is this I lead!
> Ripe apples drop about my head;
> The luscious clusters of the vine
> Upon my mouth do crush their wine;
> The nectarine and curious peach
> Into my hand themselves do reach;
> Stumbling on melons, as I pass,
> Insnared with flowers, I fall on grass.

from "The Garden,"
Andrew Marvell

I Saw a Man

I saw a man pursuing the horizon;
Round and round they sped
I was disturbed at this;
I accosted the man.
"It is futile," I said,
"You can never—"
"You lie," he cried.
And ran on.

Stephen Crane

Loveliest of Trees, the Cherry Now

Loveliest of trees, the cherry now
Is hung with bloom along the bough,
And stands about the woodland ride
Wearing white for Eastertide.

Now, of my threescore years and ten,
Twenty will not come again,
And take from seventy springs a score,
It only leaves me fifty more.

And since to look at things in bloom
Fifty springs are little room,
Above the woodlands I will go
To see the cherry hung with snow.

A. E. Housman

GOING HOME

If you cannot wait to get home then you will find this section reassuring,
but these poems could make all the difference on those days when home
is definitely not where the heart is. Frost's poem takes the philosophical
approach to resisting temptation, while the Dennis O'Driscoll and the
Wendy Cope poems are reminders of the more practical delights of home.

Home

when all is said and done
what counts is having someone
you can phone at five to ask

for the immersion heater
to be switched to "bath"
and the pizza taken from the deepfreeze

Dennis O'Driscoll

Stopping by Woods on a Snowy Evening

Whose woods these are I think I know.
His house is in the village, though;
He will not see me stopping here
To watch his woods fill up with snow.

My little horse must think it queer
To stop without a farmhouse near
Between the woods and frozen lake
The darkest evening of the year.

He gives his harness bells a shake
To ask if there is some mistake.
The only other sound's the sweep
Of easy wind and downy flake.

The woods are lovely, dark, and deep,
But I have promises to keep,
And miles to go before I sleep,
And miles to go before I sleep.

Robert Frost

Being Boring

"May you live in interesting times." *Chinese curse.*

If you ask me "What's new?," I have nothing to say
Except that the garden is growing.
I had a slight cold but it's better today.
I'm content with the way things are going.
Yes, he is the same as he usually is,
Still eating and sleeping and snoring.
I get on with my work. He gets on with his.
I know this is all very boring.

There was drama enough in my turbulent past:
Tears and passion—I've used up a tankful.
No news is good news, and long may it last,
If nothing much happens, I'm thankful.
A happier cabbage you never did see,
My vegetable spirits are soaring.
If you're after excitement, steer well clear of me.
I want to go on being boring.

I don't go to parties. Well, what are they for,
If you don't need to find a new lover?
You drink and you listen and drink a bit more
And you take the next day to recover.
Someone to stay home with was all my desire
And, now that I've found a safe mooring,
I've just one ambition in life: I aspire
To go on and on being boring.

Wendy Cope

ONE FOR THE ROAD

Drinking in moderation is now officially good for you, though if you get to the stage that Philip Larkin describes you may have taken the health thing too far.

Reflection on Ice-Breaking

Candy
Is dandy
But liquor
Is quicker.

Ogden Nash

Party Politics

I never remember holding a full drink.
    My first look shows the level half-way down.
What next? Ration the rest, and try to think
    Of higher things, until mine host comes round?

Some people say, best show an empty glass:
    Someone will fill it. Well, I've tried that too.
You may get drunk, or dry half-hours may pass.
    It seems to turn on where you are. Or who.

Philip Larkin

BEHAVING BADLY

If at this stage of the evening you are still struggling with your conscience, you should probably turn to the "Going Home" section, and save yourself a great deal of anguish. But if you've gone too far to turn back, then live for the moment. As these poems show, you are in good company.

First Fig

My candle burns at both ends;
　It will not last the night;
But ah, my foes, and o, my friends—
　It gives a lovely light!

Edna St. Vincent Millay

Symphony Recital

I do not like my state of mind;
I'm bitter, querulous, unkind.
I hate my legs, I hate my hands,
I do not yearn for lovelier lands.
I dread the dawn's recurrent light;
I have to go to bed at night.
I snoot at simple, earnest folk.
I cannot take the gentlest joke.
I find no peace in paint or type.
My world is but a lot of tripe.
I'm disillusioned, empty-breasted.
I am not sick, I am not well.
My quondam dreams are shot to hell.
My soul is crushed, my spirit sore;
I do not like me any more.
I cavil, quarrel, grumble, grouse.
I ponder on the narrow house.
I shudder at the thought of men . . .
I'm due to fall in love again.

Dorothy Parker

Gray

I have a friend
who is turning gray,
not just her hair,
and I do not know
why this is so.

Is it a lack of vitamin E
pantothenic acid, or B-12?
Or is it from being frantic
and alone?

"How long does it take you to love someone?"
I ask her.
"A hot second," she replies.
"And how long do you love them?"
"Oh, anywhere up to several months."
"And how long does it take you
to get over loving them?"
"Three weeks," she said, "tops."

Did I mention I am also
turning gray?
It is because I *adore* this woman
who thinks of love
in this way.

Alice Walker

The Longest Journey

I never was attached to that great sect,
Whose doctrine is, that each one should select
Out of the crowd a mistress or a friend,
And all the rest, though fair and wise, commend
To cold oblivion, though it is in the code
Of modern morals, and the beaten road
Which those poor slaves with weary footsteps tread,
Who travel to their home among the dead
By the broad highway of the world, and so
With one chained friend, perhaps a jealous foe,
The dreariest and the longest journey go.

from *Epipsychidion,*
Percy Bysshe Shelley

GOING TO BED

Forget Ann Summers or Viagra—nothing works faster on a flagging libido than the right poem. Try reading the e. e. cummings poem aloud, it is the perfect precoital snack. The Hugo Williams poem should be read by every man who has ever asked, "How was it for you?" and the Henry Normal poem is for anyone who has let a gym membership lapse.

may i feel

may i feel said he
(i'll squeal said she
just once said he)
it's fun said she

(may i touch said he
how much said she
a lot said he)
why not said she

(let's go said he
not too far said she
what's too far said he
where you are said she)

may i stay said he
(which way said she
like this said he
if you kiss said she

may i move said he
is it love said she)
if you're willing said he
(but you're killing said she

but it's life said he
but your wife said she
now said he)
ow said she

(tiptop said he
don't stop said she
oh no said he)
go slow said she

(cccome?said he
ummm said she)
you're divine!said he
(you are Mine said she)

e. e. cummings

Rhetorical Questions

How do you think I feel
when you make me talk to you
and won't let me stop
till the words turn into a moan?
Do you think I mind
when you put your hand over my mouth
and tell me not to move
so you can "hear" it happening?

And how do you think I like it
when you tell me what to do
and your mouth opens
and you look straight through me?
Do you think I mind
when the blank expression comes
and you set off alone
down the hall of collapsing columns?

Hugo Williams

Undressing for Sex When You Feel You're Getting Fat

It's easy to tell if someone's self-conscious about being
        overweight
because when they undress for sex
they always take their trousers off
before their shirt.

Another dead giveaway
is the futile attempt to hold their stomach in
whilst trying to pull off their socks.

With practise what usually happens is this—
firstly they make a bee-line for the side of the bed away from
the bedside lamp. Then back turned to both
the light and their partner
they slip down their trousers past their knees
whilst at the same time lowering themselves into the upright
        sitting
position on the edge of the bed.
Next, they step out of the trouser legs, tread off their socks,
        undo all
their shirt buttons, breath in and try in one swift movement
to discard their shirt and slip gracefully under the cover.

A complete waste of effort.
No one, but no one has a hope in Hell of ever enjoying sex
whilst trying to hold their breath.

Nevertheless, in the cold light of morning
they attempt once more to continue the deception and try
        desperately
to ooze out of bed unnoticed.

Henry Normal

cake

i wanted one life
you wanted another
we couldn't have our cake
so we ate each other.

Roger McGough

Warming Her Pearls

Next to my own skin, her pearls. My mistress
bids me wear them, warm them, until evening
when I'll brush her hair. At six, I place them
round her cool, white throat. All day I think of her,

resting in the Yellow Room, contemplating silk
or taffeta, which gown tonight? She fans herself
whilst I work willingly, my slow heat entering
each pearl. Slack on my neck, her rope.

She's beautiful. I dream about her
in my attic bed; picture her dancing
with tall men, puzzled by my faint, persistent scent
beneath her French perfume, her milky stones.

I dust her shoulders with a rabbit's foot,
watch the soft blush seep through her skin
like an indolent sigh. In her looking-glass
my red lips part as though I want to speak.

Full moon. Her carriage brings her home. I see
her every movement in my head. . . . Undressing,
taking off her jewels, her slim hand reaching
for the case, slipping naked into bed, the way

she always does. . . . And I lie here awake,
knowing the pearls are cooling even now
in the room where my mistress sleeps. All night
I feel their absence and I burn.

Carol Ann Duffy

A Small Hotel

My nipples tick
like little bombs of blood.

Someone is walking
in the yard outside.

I don't know why
Our Lord was crucified.

A really good fuck
makes me feel like custard.

Selima Hill

NOT TONIGHT

If the poems in the Going to Bed section are the equivalent of champagne and oysters, the poems in this section approximate to a nice cup of tea and a boiled egg. You can't trip the light fantastic *every* night.

Mrs Rip Van Winkle

I sank like a stone
into the still, deep waters of late middle age,
aching from head to foot.

I took up food
and gave up exercise.
It did me good.

And while he slept
I found some hobbies for myself.
Painting. Seeing the sights I'd always dreamed about:

The Leaning Tower.
The Pyramids. The Taj Mahal.
I made a little watercolour of them all.

But what was best,
what hands-down beat the rest,
was saying a none-too-fond farewell to sex.

Until the day
I came home with this pastel of Niagara
and he was sitting up in bed rattling Viagra.

Carol Ann Duffy

Scintillate

I have outlived
my youthfulness
so a quiet life for me

where once
I used to
scintillate

now I sin
till ten
past three.

Roger McGough

So We'll Go No More A-Roving

So we'll go no more a-roving
   So late into the night,
Though the heart be still as loving,
   And the moon be still as bright.

For the sword outwears its sheath,
   And the soul wears out the breast,
And the heart must pause to breathe,
   And Love itself have rest.

Though the night was made for loving,
   And the day returns too soon,
Yet we'll go no more a-roving
   By the light of the moon.

Lord Byron

Pad, Pad

I always remember your beautiful flowers
And the beautiful kimono you wore
When you sat on the couch
With that tigerish crouch
And told me you loved me no more.

What I cannot remember is how I felt when
 you were unkind
All I know is, if you were unkind now I should
 not mind.
Ah me, the power to feel exaggerated, angry and sad
The years have taken from me. Softly I go now, pad
 pad.

Stevie Smith

IN THE SMALL HOURS

The country of the small hours can be strange territory indeed—the shrugged-off irritations of the day turn by night into full-blown menaces. If you can't go back to sleep then switch on the light and read these poems; nothing is worth losing sleep over.

Reflection on the Fallibility of Nemesis

He who is ridden by a conscience
Worries about a lot of nonscience;
He without benefit of scruples
His fun and income soon quadruples.

Ogden Nash

A Warning

If when you have washed your hands you wash them again
though they are already perfectly clean,
if when you've checked you've got everything—
directions, cash, vaporizer, ticket—you go through
everything again just once more,

if when you are halfway down the street
you think you may not have locked the door
so you go back and yes, it is locked, but you wonder if
you remembered to switch the cooker off
so you go back to make sure,

I have to tell you it's likely to get worse.
Soon you won't be able to leave the house.
You will cram your bag with everything
you possess, you will hide it somewhere
absolutely safe.

You won't know where to put yourself.
You won't know what to do with your hands
so you'll steep them in pure bleach
but they are still offensive
so you pick up a knife.

You have lost your tongue. You have lost
your head. The cooker turns itself on
automatically, the burners are red-hot,
the warning light flashes
the sirens go off.

Dorothy Nimmo

House Fear

Always—I tell you this they learned—
Always at night when they returned
To the lonely house from far away,
To lamps unlighted and fire gone gray,
They learned to rattle the lock and key
To give whatever might chance to be,
Warning and time to be off in flight:
And preferring the out- to the indoor night,
They learned to leave the house door wide
Until they had lit the lamp inside.

Robert Frost

Cowards

Cowards die many times before their deaths:
The valiant never taste of death but once.
Of all the wonders that I yet have heard,
It seems to me most strange that men should fear;
Seeing that death, a necessary end,
Will come, when it will come.

from *Julius Caesar,* Act II, Scene II,
William Shakespeare

EARLY MORNING

Three poems for the mornings when you wake up far too early with
WHAT HAVE I DONE? written in letters of fire across your conscience.
Read the James Fenton poem when the adrenaline rush subsides, and learn
to profit from your mistake.

Story of a Hotel Room

Thinking we were safe—insanity!
We went in to make love. All the same
Idiots to trust the little hotel bedroom.
Then in the gloom . . .
. . . And who does not know that pair of shutters
With the awkward hook on them
All screeching whispers? Very well then, in the gloom
We set about acquiring one another
Urgently! But on a temporary basis
Only as guests—just guests of one another's senses.

But idiots to feel so safe you hold back nothing
Because the bed of cold, electric linen
Happens to be illicit . . .
To make love as well as that is ruinous.

Londoner, Parisian, someone should have warned us
That without permanent intentions
You have absolutely no protection
—If the act is clean, authentic, sumptuous,
The concurring deep love of the heart
Follows the naked work, profoundly moved by it.

Rosemary Tonks

Permissive Society

Wake, for the dawn has put the stars to flight,
    And in my bed a stranger: so once more,
What seemed to be a good idea last night
    Appears, this morning, sober, rather poor.

Connie Bensley

The Mistake

With the mistake your life goes in reverse.
Now you can see exactly what you did
Wrong yesterday and wrong the day before
And each mistake leads back to something worse

And every nuance of your hypocrisy
Towards yourself and every excuse
Stands solidly on the perspective lines
And there is perfect visibility.

What an enlightenment. The colonnade
Rolls past on either side. You needn't move.
The statues of your errors brush your sleeve.
You watch the tale turn back—and you're dismayed.

And this dismay at this, this big mistake
Is made worse by the sight of all those who
Knew all along where these mistakes would lead—
Those frozen friends who watched the crisis break.

Why didn't they say? Oh, but they did indeed—
said with a murmur when the time was wrong
Or by a mild refusal to assent
Or told you plainly but you would not heed.

Yes, you can hear them now. It hurts. It's worse
Than any sneer from any enemy.
Take this dismay. Lay claim to this mistake.
Look straight along the lines of this reverse.

James Fenton

WEDDINGS

The ideal poem for reading at a wedding should be touching but not too gushing—after all, it is probably going to be read by a friend or relative—and short. I think these fit the bill and they have the value of novelty. (For more suggestions see my previous anthology, *101 Poems That Could Save Your Life.*)

Now You Will Feel No Rain

Now you will feel no rain,
for each of you will be a shelter to the other.

Now you will feel no cold,
for each of you will be warmth to the other.

Now there is no loneliness for you;
now there is no more loneliness.

Now you are two bodies,
but there is only one life before you.

Go now to your dwelling place,
to enter into your days together.

And may your days be good
and long on the earth.

Apache song,
translator unknown

The Love of God, Unutterable and Perfect

The love of God, unutterable and perfect,
      flows into a pure soul the way that light
      rushes into a transparent object.
The more love that it finds, the more it gives
      itself; so that, as we grow clear and open,
      the more complete the joy of loving is.
And the more souls who resonate together,
      the greater the intensity of their love,
      for, mirror-like, each soul reflects the others.

from *The Divine Comedy,*
Dante,
translated by Stephen Mitchell

As I Dig for Wild Orchids

As I dig for wild orchids
in the autumn fields,
it is the deeply-bedded root
that I desire,
not the flower.

Izumi Shikibu,
translated by Jane Hirshfield with Mariko Aratani

FUNERALS

There are times when, sadly, we all need to find public expressions of private grief. These readings could be used at a funeral or in a letter of condolence. The right words in the right order can be a great consolation.

To everything there is a season, and a time to every purpose under the heaven: a time to be born and a time to die; a time to plant, and a time to pluck up that which is planted; a time to kill, and a time to heal; a time to break down, and a time to build up; a time to weep and a time to laugh; a time to mourn, and a time to dance; a time to cast away stones, and a time to gather stones together; a time to embrace, and a time to refrain from embracing; a time to seek, and a time to lose; a time to keep, and a time to cast away; a time to rend, and a time to sew; a time to keep silence, and a time to speak; a time to love, and a time to hate; a time for war, and a time for peace.

from *Ecclesiastes,*
Chapter 3, Verses 1–8

If I Should Go Before the Rest of You

If I should go before the rest of you,
Break not a flower nor inscribe a stone.
Nor when I'm gone speak in a Sunday voice,
But be the usual selves that I have known.
Weep if you must,
Parting is hell,
But life goes on,
So sing as well.

Joyce Grenfell

High Flight (An Airman's Ecstasy)

Oh, I have slipped the surly bonds of earth
And danced the skies on laughter-silvered wings;
Sunward I've climbed and joined the tumbling mirth
Of sun-split clouds—and done a hundred things
You have not dreamed of; wheeled and soared and swung
High in the sun-lit silence. Hovering there
I've chased the shouting wind along, and flung
My eager craft through footless halls of air;
Up, up the long, delirious, burning blue
I've topped the wind-swept heights with easy grace,
Where never lark nor even eagle flew;
And while, with silent lifting mind I've trod
The high untrespassed sanctity of space,
Put out my hand, and touched the face of God.

John Gillespie Magee

CHRISTMAS

Harassed parents who have stayed up until two A.M. in order to fill the children's stockings, only to be woken at five A.M. by said progeny, should read Wendy Cope's "A Christmas Poem" and count their blessings. "Reindeer Rap" would make a great party piece for a precocious child, much shorter than the ubiquitous and interminable "Night Before Christmas."

Reindeer Rap

Chimneys: colder.
Flightpaths: busier.
Driver: Christmas (F)
Still baffled by postcodes.

Children: more
And stay up later.
Presents: heavier.
Pay: frozen.

Mission in spite
Of all this
Accomplished.

U. A. Fanthorpe

A Christmas Poem

At Christmas little children sing and merry bells jingle,
The cold winter air makes our hands and faces tingle
And happy families go to church and cheerily they mingle
And the whole business is unbelievably dreadful, if you're
     single.

Wendy Cope

INDEX OF AUTHORS

ADCOCK, FLEUR
For a Five-Year-Old 75
AMICHAI, YEHUDA
Quick and Bitter 85
AMIS, KINGSLEY
Ye Wearie Wayfarer 55
AMMONS, A. R.
Mountain Talk 71
ATWOOD, MARGARET
Siren Song 62
BECKETT, SAMUEL
I Would Like My Love to Die 46
BENNETT, ARNOLD
*You Wake Up in the
Morning* 4
BENSLEY, CONNIE
Permissive Society 121
BETJEMAN, JOHN
Meditation on the A30 15
BLAKE, WILLIAM
Love's Secret 65
BORGES, JORGE LUIS
Since That Day 81
BROWNING, ROBERT
Pippa's Song 1
BYRON, GEORGE GORDON,
LORD
So We'll Go No More A-Roving
112
Extract from *Childe Harold's
Pilgrimage* 16

CAVAFY, C. P.
The City 56
Ithaca 70
CHENG, LIU
Poem Without a Category 20
CLANCHY, KATE
The Rich 40
CLOUGH, ARTHUR HUGH
*Say Not the Struggle Nought
Availeth* 18
COOPER, JANE
Rent 67
COPE, WENDY
Defining the Problem 83
Being Boring 93
Tough Triolet 30
Two Cures for Love 86
A Christmas Poem 130
He Tells Her 66
As Sweet 47
CRANE, STEPHEN
I Saw a Man 89
CUMMINGS, E. E.
may i feel 101
DANTE
Extract from *The Divine Comedy*
124
DESNOS, ROBERT
Last Poem 50
DICKINSON, EMILY
Friends 29

DUFFY, CAROL ANN
  Warming Her Pearls 107
  Mrs Rip Van Winkle 110
EWART, GAVIN
  Office Friendships 24
FEE, YVONNE M.
  Four o'Clock Fantasy 8
U. A. FANTHORPE
  Reindeer Rap 129
JAMES FENTON
  The Mistake 122
JAMES FENTON AND JOHN
FULLER
  The Ape at the End of the Phone
    36
FROST, ROBERT
  A Time to Talk 28
  *Stopping by Woods on a Snowy
    Evening* 92
  House Fear 117
GIBRAN, KAHLIL
  On Children from *The Prophet*
    74
GORDON, ADAM LINDSAY
  Man's Testament 54
GRAHAM, HARRY
  Common Sense 57
GRENFELL, JOYCE
  *If I Should Go Before the Rest
    of You* 127
HANNAH, SOPHIE
  Leaving and Leaving You 49
  The Pros and the Cons 51
  The Keyboard and the Mouse
    43
  *To Whom It May Concern at the
    Whalley Range Driving Test
    Centre* 13

HERRICK, ROBERT
  Love Is a Circle 41
HILL, SELIMA
  A Small Hotel 109
HOOD, THOMAS
  Extract from *A Lay of Real Life*
    27
HORACE
  Moderation from *Odes, Book II*
    39
HOUSMAN, A. E.
  Loveliest of Trees, the Cherry Now
    90
KEATS, JOHN
  Ode on Melancholy 25
KIPLING, RUDYARD
  Extract from *Sestina of the
    Tramp-Royal* 6
LARKIN, PHILIP
  Days 5
  Party Politics 96
LAWRENCE, D. H.
  Piano 60
LOGUE, CHRISTOPHER
  *To a Friend in Search of Rural
    Seclusion* 72
LOWELL, ROBERT
  Will Not Come Back 45
MCGOUGH, ROGER
  A Joy to Be Old 11
  cake 106
  Scintillate 111
MAGEE, JOHN GILLESPIE
  *High Flight (An Airman's
    Ecstasy)* 128
MARVELL, ANDREW
  Extract from *The
    Garden* 88

MEREDITH, WILLIAM
  Parents 58
MILLAY, EDNA ST. VINCENT
  First Fig 97
  Travel 69
  Dirge Without Music 78
  Time Does Not Bring Relief 82
  Feast 9
MORRISON, BLAKE
  Against Dieting 7
NASH, OGDEN
  I Would Live All My Life in
    Nonchalance and Insouciance
    38
  Reflection on Ice-Breaking 95
  Reflection on the Fallibility of
    Nemesis 114
NIMMO, DOROTHY
  A Warning 115
  My Way 61
NORMAL, HENRY
  Undressing for Sex When You
    Feel You're Getting Fat 104
O'DRISCOLL, DENNIS
  No, Thanks 31
  Home 91
  Success Story 22
PARKER, DOROTHY
  One Perfect Rose 64
  Symphony Recital 98
PLATH, SYLVIA
  Mirror 10
ROETHKE, THEODORE
  Dolor 21
ROLLINSON, NEIL
  Helpline 34
RUMENS, CAROL
  A Woman of a Certain Age 33

RUMI
  The Minute I Heard My First
    Love Story 44
SHAKESPEARE, WILLIAM
  Cowards 118
SHELLEY, PERCY BYSSHE
  The Longest Journey from
    Epipsychidion 100
SHIKIBU, IZUMI
  As I Dig for Wild Orchids 125
SIDNEY, SIR PHILIP
  The Bargain 42
SMITH, STEVIE
  I Do Not Speak 17
  Pad, Pad 113
STEVENSON, ANNE
  The Mother 73
STUBBS, JOHN HEATH
  A Charm Against the Toothache
    80
TENNYSON, ALFRED, LORD
  Extract from *Ulysses* 12
THOMAS, R. S.
  Extract from *Lore* 19
TONKS, ROSEMARY
  Story of a Hotel Room 119
WALKER, ALICE
  Gray 99
WILLIAMS, HUGO
  Rhetorical Questions
    103
  All That 84
  Siren Song 53
WORDSWORTH, WILLIAM
  My Heart Leaps Up When I
    Behold 3
YEATS, W. B.
  When You Are Old 87

YUNG, SHAO
*Song on Being Too Lazy to
Get Up* 2

OTHERS
Now You Will Feel No Rain,
Apache song 123

Extract from *Ecclesiastes*,
Chapter 3, Verses 1–8 126
"Here Lies the Man Richard,"
epitaph, Chelmsford
Cathedral, Essex 68
Children, Anonymous 76
*Westron Wind, When Will Thou
Blow*, Anonymous 48

EMOTIONAL INDEX

Getting Out of Bed
"*Pippa's Song,*" Robert Browning 1
"*Song on Being Too Lazy to Get Up,*" Shao Yung 2
"*My Heart Leaps Up When I Behold,*" William Wordsworth 3
"*You Wake Up in the Morning,*" Arnold Bennett 4
"*Days,*" Philip Larkin 5
Extract from "*Sestina of the Tramp-Royal,*" Rudyard Kipling 6

Stepping on the Scale
"*Against Dieting,*" Blake Morrison 7
"*Four o'Clock Fantasy*" Yvonne M. Fee 8
"*Feast,*" Edna St. Vincent Millay 9

The Mirror Moment
"*Mirror,*" Sylvia Plath 10
"*A Joy to Be Old,*" Roger McGough 11
Extract from *Ulysses,* Alfred Lord Tennyson 12

Drivetime
"*To Whom It May Concern at the Whalley Range Driving Test Centre,*" Sophie Hannah 13
"*Meditation on the A30,*" John Betjeman 15

Theme Songs
Extract from *Childe Harold's Pilgrimage,* Lord Byron 16
"*I Do Not Speak,*" Stevie Smith 17
"*Say Not the Struggle Nought Availeth,*" Arthur Hugh Clough 18
Extract from "*Lore,*" R. S. Thomas 19

Office Politics
"*Poem Without a Category,*" Liu Cheng 20
"*Dolor,*" Theodore Roethke 21
"*Success Story,*" Dennis O'Driscoll 22
"*Office Friendships,*" Gavin Ewart 24

Blue Period
"*Ode on Melancholy,*" John Keats 25

Friends Like These
Extract from "*A Lay of Real Life,*" Thomas Hood 27
"*A Time to Talk,*" Robert Frost 28
"*Friends,*" Emily Dickinson 29

Just Say No
"*Tough Triolet (for David Mason),*" Wendy Cope 30

"*No, Thanks,*" Dennis O'Driscoll
31

"*A Woman of a Certain Age,*" Carol
Rumens 33

System Not Responding

"*Helpline,*" Neil Rollinson 34

"*The Ape at the End of the Phone,*"
James Fenton and John Fuller
36

Credit Lines

"*I Would Live All My Life in
Nonchalance and Insouciance,*"
Ogden Nash 38

"*Moderation,*" Horace, *Odes, Book
II,* translated by William
Cowper 39

"*The Rich,*" Kate Clanchy 40

Love Struck

"*Love Is a Circle,*" Robert Herrick
41

"*The Bargain,*" Sir Philip Sidney
42

"*The Keyboard and the Mouse,*"
Sophie Hannah 43

"*The Minute I Heard My First Love
Story,*" Rumi, translated by
Coleman Barks with John
Moyne 44

"*Will Not Come Back,*" Robert
Lowell 45

"*I Would Like My Love to Die,*"
Samuel Beckett 46

"*As Sweet,*" Wendy Cope 47

Separated from the One You Love

"*Westron Wind, When Will Thou
Blow,*" Anon. 48

"*Leaving and Leaving You,*" Sophie
Hannah 49

"*Last Poem,*" Robert Desnos,
translated from the French by
X. J. Kennedy 50

Call Waiting

"*The Pros and the Cons,*" Sophie
Hannah 51

"*Siren Song,*" Hugo Williams 53

Prescriptions for Life

"*Man's Testament,*" Adam Lindsay
Gordon 54

"*Ye Wearie Wayfarer,*" Kingsley
Amis 55

"*The City,*" C. P. Cavafy, translated
by Edmund Keeley and Philip
Sherrard 56

"*Common Sense,*" Harry Graham
57

The Parent Trap

"*Parents,*" William Meredith 58

"*Piano,*" D. H. Lawrence 60

"*My Way,*" Dorothy Nimmo 61

Battle of the Sexes

"*Siren Song,*" Margaret Atwood 62

"*One Perfect Rose,*" Dorothy
Parker 64

"*Love's Secret,*" William Blake 65

"*He Tells Her,*" Wendy Cope 66

"*Rent,*" Jane Cooper 67

"*Here Lies the Man Richard,*" epitaph, Chelmsford Cathedral, Essex 68

Escape Routes
"*Travel,*" Edna St. Vincent Millay 69
"*Ithaca,*" C. P. Cavafy, translated by Edmund Keeley and Philip Sherrard 70
"*Mountain Talk,*" A. R. Ammons 71
"*To a Friend in Search of Rural Seclusion,*" Christopher Logue 72

Off to School
"*The Mother,*" Anne Stevenson 73
"*On Children,*" from *The Prophet* by Kahlil Gibran 74
"*For a Five-Year-Old,*" Fleur Adcock 75
"*Children,*" Anonymous 76

Gone Forever
"*Dirge Without Music,*" Edna St. Vincent Millay 78

Toothache
"*A Charm Against the Toothache,*" John Heath Stubbs 80

Breaking Up Is Hard to Do
"*Since That Day,*" Jorge Luis Borges 81
"*Time Does Not Bring Relief,*" Edna St. Vincent Millay 82

"*Defining the Problem,*" Wendy Cope 83
"*All That,*" Hugo Williams 84
"*Quick and Bitter,*" Yehuda Amichai, translated from the Hebrew by Assia Gutmann 85
"*Two Cures for Love,*" Wendy Cope 86
"*When You Are Old,*" W. B. Yeats 87

Take 5
Extract from "*The Garden,*" Andrew Marvell 88
"*I Saw a Man,*" Stephen Crane 89
"*Loveliest of Trees, the Cherry Now,*" A. E. Housman 90

Going Home
"*Home,*" Dennis O'Driscoll 91
"*Stopping by Woods on a Snowy Evening,*" Robert Frost 92
"*Being Boring,*" Wendy Cope 93

One for the Road
"*Reflection on Ice-Breaking,*" Ogden Nash 95
"*Party Politics,*" Philip Larkin 96

Behaving Badly
"*First Fig,*" Edna St. Vincent Millay 97
"*Symphony Recital,*" Dorothy Parker 98
"*Gray,*" Alice Walker 99

"*The Longest Journey*" from
  Epipsychidion, Percy Bysshe
  Shelley 100

Going to Bed

"*may i feel,*" e. e. cummings 101
"*Rhetorical Questions,*" Hugo
  Williams 103
"*Undressing for Sex When You Feel
  You're Getting Fat,*" Henry
  Normal 104
"*cake,*" Roger McGough 106
"*Warming Her Pearls,*" Carol Ann
  Duffy 107
"*A Small Hotel,*" Selima Hill 109

Not Tonight

"*Mrs Rip Van Winkle,*" Carol Ann
  Duffy 110
"*Scintillate,*" Roger McGough 111
"*So We'll Go No More A-Roving,*"
  Lord Byron 112
"*Pad, Pad,*" Stevie Smith 113

In the Small Hours

"*Reflection on the Fallibility of
  Nemesis,*" Ogden Nash 114
"*A Warning,*" Dorothy Nimmo
  115
"*House Fear,*" Robert Frost 117
"*Cowards,*" William Shakespeare
  118

Early Morning

"*Story of a Hotel Room,*" Rosemary
  Tonks 119
"*Permissive Society,*" Connie
  Bensley 121
"*The Mistake,*" James Fenton 122

Weddings

"*Now You Will Feel No Rain,*"
  Apache song 123
Extract from *The Divine Comedy,*
  Dante 124
"*As I Dig for Wild Orchids,*" Izumi
  Shikibu translated by Jane
  Hirshfield with Mariko Aratani
  125

Funerals

Extract from *Ecclesiastes,* Chapter
  3, Verses 1–8 126
"*If I Should Go Before the Rest of
  You,*" Joyce Grenfell 127
"*High Flight (An Airman's
  Ecstasy),*" John Gillespie Magee
  128

Christmas

"*Reindeer Rap,*" U. A. Fanthorpe
  129
"*A Christmas Poem,*" Wendy
  Cope 130

We are grateful for permission to reprint the following copyright poems in this collection:

Extracts from the *Authorized Version of the Bible* (King James Bible), the rights of which are vested in the Crown, are reproduced by permission of the Crown's Patentee, Cambridge University Press.

Fleur Adcock: "For a Five-Year-Old," from *Poems 1960–2000* (2000), reprinted by permission of the publisher, Bloodaxe Books.

Yehuda Amichai: "Quick and Bitter," translated by Assia Gutmann from *Poems of Jerusalem and Love Poems* (Sheep Meadow Press), reprinted by permission of the publishers.

Kingsley Amis: "Ye Wearie Wayfarer" ("Life is largely grief and labour"), copyright © 2000 by Kingsley Amis, from *Experience*, by Martin Amis, reprinted by permission of Jonathan Clowes Ltd., London, on behalf of the Literary Estate of Sir Kingsley Amis.

A. R. Ammons: "Mountain Talk," from *Collected Poems 1951–1971* (W.W. Norton & Company, 1972), copyright © 1972 by A. R. Ammons, reprinted by permission of W.W. Norton & Company, Inc.

Margaret Atwood: "Siren Song," from *Selected Poems 1965–1975* (Virago, 1975), reprinted by permission of the publishers, Time Warner Books UK, Houghton Mifflin Company, and Oxford University Press, Canada.

Samuel Beckett: "I Would Like My Love to Die," from *Collected Poems* (Calder, 1984), reprinted by permission of Calder Publications Ltd.

Arnold Bennett: "You Wake Up in the Morning," reprinted by permission of A. P. Watt on behalf of Madame V. M. Eldin.

Connie Bensley: "Permissive Society," from *Central Reservations* (1990), reprinted by permission of the publisher, Bloodaxe Books.

John Betjeman: "Meditation on the A30," from *Collected Poems* (1978), reprinted by permission of the publishers, John Murray (Publishers) Ltd.

Jorge Luis Borges: "Since That Day," copyright holder not traced.

C. P. Cavafy: "The City" and "Valedictory" ("Ithaca"), from *The Collected Poems,* translated by Edmund Keeley and Philip Sherrard, edited by George Savidis (The Hogarth Press, 1984), copyright © The Estate of C. P. Cavafy 1975, reprinted by permission of The Random House Group Ltd. and Rogers, Coleridge & White Ltd., 20 Powis Mews, London W11 1JN, on behalf of the Estate of C. P. Cavafy.

Liu Cheng: "Poem Without a Category," from *The Columbia Book of Chinese Poetry* (Columbia University Press, 1984), translated and edited by Burton Watson, copyright © 1984 Columbia University Press, reprinted by permission of the publisher.

Kate Clanchy: "The Rich," from *Samarkand* (Picador, 1999), reprinted by permission of Macmillan, London, UK.

Jane Cooper: "Rent," from *The Flashboat: Poems Collected and Reclaimed* (W.W. Norton & Company, Inc., 2000), copyright © 2000 by Jane Cooper, reprinted by permission of the author and the publishers.

Wendy Cope: "Two Cures for Love," "Defining the Problem," and "As Sweet," from *Serious Concerns* (1992), "A Christmas Poem," from *Making Cocoa for Kingsley Amis* (1986), and "Being Boring," and "He Tells Her," from *If I Don't Know* (2001), reprinted by permission of the publishers, Faber & Faber Ltd., and of PFD on behalf of the author; "Tough Triolet (for David Mason)" reprinted by permission of the author.

e. e. cummings: "may i feel said he," from *Complete Poems 1904–1962*, edited by George J. Firmage, copyright © 1991 by the Trustees for the e. e. cummings Trust and George James Firmage, reprinted by permission of the publishers, W.W. Norton & Company, Inc.

Dante: lines from *The Divine Comedy*, translated by Stephen Mitchell in *The Enlightened Heart: An Anthology of Sacred Poetry*, edited by S. Mitchell (HarperCollins Publishers, Inc.), copyright © Stephen Mitchell 1989, reprinted by permission of the publishers.

Robert Desnos: "Last Poem," translated by X. J. Kennedy from Willis Barnstone et al. (eds.): *Modern European Poetry* (Bantam Books, 1966), reprinted by permission of Curtis Brown Ltd., New York.

Emily Dickinson: "They Might Not Need Me," from *The Poems of Emily Dickinson*, edited by Ralph W. Franklin (The Belknap Press of Harvard University Press), copyright © 1998 by the President and Fellows of Harvard College, copyright © 1951, 1955, 1979 by the President and Fellows of Harvard College, reprinted by permission of the publishers and the Trustees of Amherst College.

Carol Ann Duffy: "Warming Her Pearls," from *Selling Manhattan* (1987), reprinted by permission of Anvil Press Poetry Ltd.; "Mrs Rip Van Winkle," from *The World's Wife* (Picador), reprinted by permission of Macmillan, London, UK.

Gavin Ewart: "Office Friendships," from *The Collected Ewart 1933–1980* (Hutchinson, 1980), reprinted by permission of Margo Ewart.

U. A. Fanthorpe: "Reindeer Rap," copyright © U. A. Fanthorpe 1982, from *Standing To* (1982), reprinted by permission of Peterloo Poets.

Yvonne M. Fee: "Four O'Clock Fantasy," copyright © Yvonne M. Fee 1997, first published in *Eating Your Cake and Having It*, edited by Ann Gray (Fatchance Press, 1997), reprinted by permission of the author.

James Fenton: "The Mistake," from *Manila Envelope* (Faber, 1989), copyright © James Fenton 1989, reprinted by permission of PFD on behalf of the author.

James Fenton and John Fuller: "The Ape at the End of the Phone," from *Partingtime Hall* (Penguin, 1987), copyright © James Fenton and John Fuller 1987, reprinted by permission of PFD on behalf of the authors.

Robert Frost: "A Time to Talk," "Stopping by Woods on a Snowy Evening" and "House Fear," from *The Poetry of Robert Frost*, edited by Edward Connery Lathem (Henry Holt & Company/Jonathan Cape), copyright 1916, 1923, 1944, 1951, © 1969 by Robert Frost, reprinted by permission of the Estate of Robert Frost and the publishers, The Random House Group Ltd. and Henry Holt & Company, LLC.

Joyce Grenfell: "If I Should Go Before the Rest of You," from *Turn Back the Clock* (Futura, 1977), copyright © Joyce Grenfell 1977, reprinted by permission of Sheil Land Associates Ltd.

Sophie Hannah: "Leaving and Leaving You," from *Leaving and Leaving You* (1999); "The Keyboard and the Mouse," from *The Hero and the Girl Next Door* (1995); "The Pros and Cons" and "To Whom it May Concern at the Whalley Range Driving Test Centre," from *Hotels Like Houses* (1996), all reprinted by permission of the publisher, Carcanet Press Ltd.

John Heath-Stubbs: "A Charm Against the Toothache," from *Collected Poems* (Carcanet, 1988), reprinted by permission of David Higham Associates.

Selima Hill: "A Small Hotel," from *A Little Book of Meat* (1993), reprinted by permission of the publisher, Bloodaxe Books.

A. E. Housman: "Loveliest of Trees, the Cherry Now…," from *A Shropshire Lad*, reprinted by permission of The Society of Authors and the literary representative of the Estate of A. E. Housman.

Ogden Nash: "Introspective Reflection" (I would live all my life in nonchalance and insouciance), copyright © 1930 by Ogden Nash, renewed, "Reflection on Ice-Breaking," copyright © 1930 by Ogden Nash, renewed, and "Reflection on the Fallibility of Nemesis," copyright © 1931 by Ogden Nash, renewed, from *Candy Is Dandy: The Best of Ogden Nash*, reprinted by permission of Curtis Brown Ltd., New York, and the publishers, Andre Deutsch Ltd.

Dorothy Nimmo: "A Warning," from *Children's Games* (Giant Step, 1998), and "My Way," from *Homewards* (Giant Steps, 1987), both reprinted by permission of the Margaret Nimmo Estate.

Henry Normal: "Undressing for Sex When You Feel You're Getting Fat," from *Nude Modelling for the Afterlife* (1993), copyright © Henry Normal 1993, reprinted by permission of the publisher, Bloodaxe Books, and of the author c/o ICM, London.

Dennis O'Driscoll: "Home" and "Success Story," from *Quality Time* (1997), reprinted by permission of Anvil Press Poetry Ltd.; "No Thanks," first published in the *TLS*, January 7, 2000, reprinted by permission of the author.

Dorothy Parker: "One Perfect Rose" and "Symptom Recital," from *The Collected Dorothy Parker* (1973), reprinted by permission of the publisher, Gerald Duckworth & Co. Ltd.; also from *Dorothy Parker: Complete Poems*, copyright ©1999 by The National Association for the Advancement of Colored People, reprinted by permission of Penguin, a division of Penguin Putnam Inc.

Sylvia Plath: "Mirror," first published in *The New Yorker*, from *Collected Poems* (1971), reprinted by permission of the publishers, Faber & Faber Ltd.; also from *Crossing the Water*, copyright © 1963 by Ted Hughes, reprinted by permission of HarperCollins Publishers, Inc.

Theodore Roethke: "Dolor," copyright © 1943 by Modern Poetry Association, Inc., from *The Collected Poems of Theodore Roethke* (1966), reprinted by permission of the publishers, Faber & Faber Ltd. and Doubleday, a division of Random House, Inc.

Neil Rollinson: "Helpline," from *Spanish Fly* (Jonathan Cape, 2001), reprinted by permission of the author and The Random House Publishing Group.

Carol Rumens: "A Woman of a Certain Age," from *Selected Poems* (Chatto & Windus, 1987), copyright © Carol Rumens 1987, reprinted by permission of PFD on behalf of Carol Rumens.

X. J. Kennedy translation of Robert Desnos: "Last Poem," from Willis Barnstone et al. (eds.): *Modern European Poetry* (Bantam Books, 1966), reprinted by permission of Curtis Brown Ltd., New York.

Rudyard Kipling: extract from "Sestina of the Tramp-Royal," from *Rudyard Kipling's Verse: The Definitive Edition* (Hodder & Stoughton, 1945), by permission of A. P. Watt Ltd. on behalf of The National Trust for Places of Historic Interest or Natural Beauty.

Philip Larkin: "Days" and "Party Politics," from *Collected Poems* (Faber, 1988), copyright © 1988, 1989 by the Estate of Philip Larkin, reprinted by permission of the publishers, Faber & Faber Ltd. and Farrar, Straus & Giroux, LLC.

Christopher Logue: "To a Friend in Search of Rural Seclusion," from *Selected Poems* (1996), reprinted by permission of the publishers, Faber & Faber Ltd. and of David Godwin Associates.

Robert Lowell: "Will Not Come Back," from *Selected Poems* (Faber, 1977), copyright © Robert Lowell 1976, reprinted by permission of the publishers, Faber & Faber Ltd and Farrar, Straus & Giroux, LLC.

Roger McGough: "A Joy to be Old," "Cake" and "Scintillate," from *Blazing Fruit: Selected Poems 1967-1987* (Penguin, 1990), copyright © Roger McGough 1990, reprinted by permission of PFD on behalf of Roger McGough.

John Gillespie Magee: "High Flight (An Airman's Ecstasy)," from *John Magee: The Pilot Poet* (1996), reprinted by permission of the publishers, This England Books, Cheltenham, UK.

William Meredith: "Parents," from *Effort at Speech: New and Selected Poems* (TriQuarterly Books/Northwestern University Press, 1997), copyright © 1997 by William Meredith, reprinted by permission of the author and the publishers. All rights reserved.

Edna St. Vincent Millay: "First Fig," "Travel," "Dirge Without Music," "Time does not bring relief" and "Feast," from *Collected Poems* (HarperCollins), copyright © 1917, 1921, 1922, 1923, 1928, 1945, 1948, 1950, 1951, 1955 by Edna St. Vincent Millay and Norma Millay Ellis, reprinted by permission of Elizabeth Barnett, Literary Executor. All rights reserved.

Blake Morrison: "Against Dieting," copyright © Blake Morrison 1999, from *Last Words: New Poetry for the New Century* edited by Don Paterson and Joe Shagcott (Picador, 1999), reprinted by permission of PFD on behalf of the author.

Rumi: "The Minute I Heard My First Love Story," from John Moyne and Coleman Barks (eds.): *Open Secret: Versions of Rumi*, originally published by Threshold Books, copyright © 1984 Threshold Books, reprinted by permission of Threshold Productions.

Izumi Shikibu: "As I Dig For Wild Orchids," from *The Ink Dark Moon: Love Poems by Ono no Kamachi and Izumi Shikibu* translated by Jane Hirschfield with Mariko Aratani, copyright © 1990 by Jane Hirschfield and Mariko Aratami, reprinted by permission of Vintage Books, a division of Random House, Inc.

Stevie Smith: "I Do Not Speak" and "Pad, Pad," from *Collected Poems of Stevie Smith* (Penguin/New Directions), copyright © Stevie Smith 1972, reprinted by permission of the James MacGibbon Estate and New Directions Publishing Corporation.

Anne Stevenson: "The Mother," from *Collected Poems 1955–1995* (2000), reprinted by permission of the publisher, Bloodaxe Books.

R. S. Thomas: Extract from "Lore," from *Selected Poems* (1986), reprinted by permission of the publisher, Bloodaxe Books.

Rosemary Tonks: "Story of a Hotel Room," from *Notes on Cafes and Bedrooms* (Putnam, 1963), copyright © Rosemary Tonks 1963, 1975, reprinted by permission of Sheil Land Associates.

Alice Walker: "Gray," from *Horses Make a Landscape More Beautiful* (Harcourt/The Women's Press), copyright © 1979 by Alice Walker, reprinted by permission of David Higham Associates and Harcourt, Inc.

Hugo Williams: "Rhetorical Questions," "All That," and "Siren Song," from *Billy's Rain* (1999), reprinted by permission of the publishers, Faber & Faber Ltd.

W. B. Yeats: "When You Are Old," from *Collected Poems* (Macmillan), reprinted by permission of A. P. Watt on behalf of Michael B. Yeats, and from *Collected Works of W. B. Yeats Volume 1: The Poems* (Revised) edited by Richard J. Finneran (Scribner, 1997), reprinted by permission of Scribner, an imprint of Simon & Schuster Adult Publishing Group.

Shao Yung: "Song on Being Too Lazy to Get Up," from *The Columbia Book of Chinese Poetry*, translated and edited by Burton Watson, copyright © 1984 Columbia University Press, reprinted by permission of the publisher.

Every effort has been made to trace and contact all copyright holders before publication. If notified, the publisher will be pleased to make any necessary arrangements at the earliest opportunity.